## Dear Parent:
## Your child's love of reading starts here!

Every child learns to read in a different way and at his or her own speed. Some go back and forth between reading levels and read favourite books again and again. Others read through each level in order. You can help your young reader improve and become more confident by encouraging his or her own interests and abilities. From books your child reads with you to the first books he or she reads alone, there are I Can Read Books for every stage of reading:

### SHARED READING
Basic language, word repetition, and whimsical illustrations, ideal for sharing with your emergent reader

### BEGINNING READING
Short sentences, familiar words, and simple concepts for children eager to read on their own

### READING WITH HELP
Engaging stories, longer sentences, and language play for developing readers

### READING ALONE
Complex plots, challenging vocabulary, and high-interest topics for the independent reader

### ADVANCED READING
Short paragraphs, chapters, and exciting themes for the perfect bridge to chapter books

I Can Read Books have introduced children to the joy of reading since 1957. Featuring award-winning authors and illustrators and a fabulous cast of beloved characters, I Can Read Books set the standard for beginning readers.

A lifetime of discovery begins with the magical words "I Can Read!"

I Can Read *Hockey Stories*

# I Can Read!

**READING 2 WITH HELP**

# HOCKEY STORIES

## BOOKS 1 TO 6

### Collins

I Can Read Book® is a trademark of HarperCollins Publishers

*Hockey Stories: Books 1 to 6*
Text copyright © 2019 by HarperCollins Publishers Ltd
Illustrations © 2019 by Nick Craine
All rights reserved.

Published by Collins, an imprint of HarperCollins Publishers Ltd

The six stories in this book were previously published by HarperCollins Publishers Ltd in
individual I Can Read editions in 2019. "The Best First Game," "The Golden Goal," "Hockey
at Home," "The Masked Man" and "What's in a Number?" are adapted from stories of the
same titles in *5-Minute Hockey Stories* by Meg Braithwaite, illustrations by Nick Craine.
"Hayley's Journey" is adapted from the story "Hayley Wickenheiser: Hockey Legend" in
*5-Minute Stories for Fearless Girls* by Sarah Howden, illustrations by Nick Craine.

HarperCollins books may be purchased for educational, business, or sales promotional use
through our Special Markets Department.

HarperCollins Publishers Ltd
Bay Adelaide Centre, East Tower
22 Adelaide Street West, 41st Floor
Toronto, Ontario, Canada
M5H 4E3

*www.harpercollins.ca*

Library and Archives Canada Cataloguing in Publication information is available upon request.

ISBN 978-1-44347-193-0

Printed and bound in Latvia
PNB 9 8 7 6 5 4 3 2 1

# CONTENTS

# THE BEST

# FIRST GAME

by Meg Braithwaite

Illustrations by Nick Craine

Auston stepped up to the plate.

The pitcher threw the ball.

Auston swung his bat.

Auston hit a home run!

Auston went up to bat again.

He hit another home run.

Auston's team won the game.

"Can you play tomorrow?"
asked Auston's baseball coach.
"Sorry, coach," said Auston.
"I have a hockey game."

Auston liked baseball.

But he was really good at

hockey too.

"Dad, I love hockey," said Auston.

"Maybe even more than baseball."

Auston smiled.

"Can I play hockey all the time?"

Auston stopped playing baseball.

Now he could play hockey every day.

Auston scored goal after goal.

He got good enough

to join the NHL.

The Toronto Maple Leafs
had first pick in the NHL draft.
They chose Auston.

It was time for Auston's
very first NHL game.
The Toronto Maple Leafs were facing
the Ottawa Senators.

The game started.

Auston skated across the ice.

Auston got his stick on the puck.

He shot it past the goalie

with a flick of his wrist.

A goal!

ONE

Auston had scored a goal!

His teammates said, "Great job!"

His parents whistled from the crowd.

But there was no time to celebrate.

The game was starting up again.

The Senators took the puck.

They tied the game quickly.

Then they scored again!

Auston skated as fast as he could

to get to the puck.

First, he pushed it through

Number 68's legs.

Then he got it for himself.

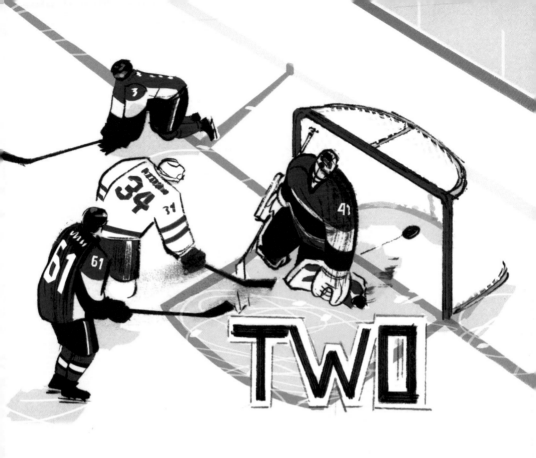

Finally, he skated toward the net
and shot the puck.
His second goal!

The second period started.

The teams were tied.

Soon, Auston got the puck again.

He was right in front of the net.

He took a shot and scored.

Three goals. Auston got a hat trick!

The crowd roared.

They threw their hats onto the ice.

Auston's mom watched from her seat.

She was so happy,

she burst into tears.

The two teams kept fighting
for the puck.

The second period was almost over.

The Senators tied the score again.

Then, something incredible happened.

Auston got the puck right before

the buzzer made

its loud buzzing sound.

Auston skated closer to the net.

He snapped the puck past the goalie!

# FOUR

The puck went right in.

His fourth goal!

Auston had done something amazing.

Other players had scored hat tricks

in their very first games.

But no one had ever scored

four goals like Auston had.

The score was tied after
the third period.

Then the game went into overtime.

And the Senators scored.

The Senators won the game

by one goal.

Auston was disappointed

that the Leafs hadn't won.

But he had broken a hockey record.

He played the best first game ever.

# THE GOLDEN GOAL

by Meg Braithwaite

Illustrations by Nick Craine

He shoots. He scores!

All goals are exciting.

But some goals are extra-special.

Some goals are golden.

In 2010, the Winter Olympic games come to Canada.

Canadian hockey fans are so excited!

They want their team to win the gold medal on home ice.

But the fans are also scared.

The men's team didn't win

a medal at the last Olympics.

This time, Team Canada makes it
to the gold medal game!
They will face the United States.

The U.S. team is very good.

They beat Team Canada

the week before.

Either team could win gold.

The puck drops!

Both teams play carefully.

They don't want to make mistakes.

But they play hard.

And fast.

Finally, Canada scores!

Now they have a 1–0 lead.

The second period

is one of the best ever.

The fans watch every move,

cheering for the home team.

Canada scores again.

Then the U.S. scores too.

When the buzzer sounds,

the score is 2–1 for Canada.

The third period starts.

Canada takes a shot.

But the puck hits the goal post.

Team Canada shoots again.

The puck misses the net.

Even Sidney Crosby can't score.

The crowd groans.

Nothing seems to be working.

There are only a few minutes left

in the game.

If Canada can stop the U.S.,

the home team will win.

Then disaster strikes.

The U.S. scores to tie the game.

The arena is silent.

The Canadian fans are shocked.

The game is going into overtime.

Team Canada is very nervous.

The fans are nervous too.

"Who will be our hero?"

asks Team Canada's coach.

The game starts again.

Players fly across the ice.

The clock ticks.

No one scores.

Sidney chases the puck.

Sidney gets the puck.

He passes it to his teammate.

Sidney skates toward the net.

He gets the puck again.

But something is wrong.

Sidney is too far away.

How can he score from there?

Sidney takes a chance.

He snaps his stick and shoots.

The puck skids between

the goalie's pads.

Sidney doesn't see the puck go in.

But he knows he's scored

by the roar of the crowd.

Canada wins!

Sidney throws his stick
and gloves in the air.
The fans cheer and shout.
A fan throws a big flag
onto the ice.

Sidney skates around the ice.

He waves the big flag.

No one will ever forget

Sidney's golden goal.

# HAYLEY'S JOURNEY

by Sarah Howden

Illustrations by Nick Craine

Hayley Wickenheiser

is seven years old.

She is skating on the ice rink

in her backyard.

It is late at night.

Hayley doesn't mind the dark.

She can feel where the puck is.

She can hear where it's going.

Hayley's dad comes outside.

"What are you doing?" he asks.

"It's pitch-black out here!"

Hayley knows he's not mad.

She can tell that he's smiling.

"I couldn't sleep," Hayley says

with a shrug.

Then she turns and shoots the puck.

Hayley is now ten.

She is on a boys' hockey team.

"I'm just as good as any boy,"

she says as she laces her skates.

But Hayley is a girl.

It can be hard being different

from her teammates.

"I think I'll tuck my hair up," Hayley says.

"Then no one will know the truth."

Hayley hopes that one day
it won't matter that she's a girl.
She hopes it will be easier
to just play the game she loves.

Hayley moves the puck down the ice.

She is quick and strong.

"Good work!" says her coach.

Hayley nods and shoots the puck.

Hayley works hard over the years.
She trains at the rink and
she trains at home.

And one day she makes it
to Team Canada.
Hayley is only fifteen years old.

Team Canada is about to play
the gold-medal game.

"Can I do this?" Hayley wonders.

Hayley looks around at the other women on her team. She used to dream of playing with them.

"You are my heroes," Hayley says.

They smile at her.

"Maybe one day I'll be a hero too,"
she thinks.

Then the game begins.

Now Hayley only thinks about

playing her best.

Hayley takes a deep breath.

And she shoots the puck.

Now Hayley is all grown up.

She is on Canada's

Olympic hockey team.

Hayley has been to the

Olympics before.

But this time is special.

This year the Olympics

are in Canada.

And Hayley is the team captain.

Team Canada has made it to
the final game.
They will play against Team USA.

Both teams are great.

Either team could win gold.

The game is about to start.

"We can do this!"

Hayley calls to her team.

The crowd roars from the stands.

Hayley gets ready.

The puck is dropped.

"I've got it!" Hayley calls.

The game is on!

Hayley has worked hard to get here.

It's been a long journey.

"We're going to win this game,"

Hayley thinks to herself.

And Hayley is right!

Team Canada wins gold.

Hayley is a true hero.

She always has been.

# HOCKEY

# AT HOME

by Meg Braithwaite

Illustrations by Nick Craine

Mario Lemieux is a big hockey star.

He has won the Stanley Cup

five times.

He has played hockey everywhere.

When Mario was a kid,

he didn't just play table hockey.

He didn't just watch hockey on TV.

He didn't just play hockey

at the rink.

What Mario did was
much more magical.

Mario's family loved hockey.

Papa loved it.

His brothers loved it.

Maybe Mama loved it most of all.

In the winter,

Papa built a rink on the front lawn.

Mario and his brothers skated on it.

They loved playing hockey on it too.

One day it was snowing very hard.

The snow covered the rink.

It was very deep.

Papa tried to clear off the ice.

Mario and his brothers helped.

But it didn't work.

"It's snowing too fast," said Mario.

Papa and the boys had to give up
and go inside.

Mario and his brothers opened

the front door.

They marched into the house.

The boys were covered in snow.
But they walked right into
the living room.

"Stop, stop," said Mama.

"Look at my carpet!"

Mario and his brothers looked down.

The carpet was covered in snow.
The snow was melting and
making wet spots.

Mario and his brothers

felt bad about the carpet.

But they were also sad.

"We want to play hockey," they said.

Mama looked at the snowy carpet.

"I have an idea," she said.

"But I'll need your help."

First, Mama turned off the heat.

Then she opened the windows.

Gusts of air filled the house.

"We have to get this place cold,"

Mama said.

Next, she opened the front door.

"And now for the snow!" Mama said.

Mama went out to the yard.

She came back with

a shovel full of snow.

Mama carried the snow
to the living room.
She dumped it on the carpet.
Mario and his brothers
couldn't believe it!

Mama brought in more snow.

And more snow.

And more.

Until the carpet was covered.

113

Then Mama used the shovel
to press the snow down.
She made the snow hard and even.
It was just like a sheet of ice.

The living room was a skating rink!

"Get your skates on!" Mama said.

Mario and his brothers played

hockey in their living room.

They skated past the sofa.

They passed the puck by the TV.

Later Mama would say,

"They really ruined my rug."

Not everyone believes the story.

But Mario remembers.

"It was the best hockey rink ever,"
Mario said.

# THE MASKED MAN

by Meg Braithwaite

Illustrations by Nick Craine

In 1959, hockey was a scary game.

NHL players didn't wear helmets.

And goalies didn't wear masks.

It was a scary time.

Players zoomed around the ice,

chasing the puck.

Goalies stood tall in net,

just waiting to block a shot.

Lots of players got hurt.
They had no protection
for their heads and faces.

Finally, one Montreal Canadien
decided he'd had enough.
Jacques Plante wanted a change.

Jacques had been a goalie for about ten years.

He'd been hurt many times.

He'd broken a lot of bones.

Jacques wanted to find a way

to protect his face.

Goalies had tried masks before.

None of them had worked.

Then something lucky happened.

One day, an inventor saw Jacques

get hit in the head with a puck.

He offered to make Jacques a mask.

The mask looked a little spooky.

But Jacques loved it.

He started to wear the mask

at every practice.

Jacques's coach did not
like the mask.

He thought goalies played better
when they were a little scared.

The coach told Jacques he couldn't wear his mask in real games. Jacques wasn't happy.

Then, during one game, a puck hit
Jacques right in the face.
It hit him really hard.

The puck cut Jacques's face and
broke his nose.

Jacques skated off the ice.

He went to the locker room.

A doctor taped Jacques's nose and
sewed up his cut.
It took seven stitches.

Then the coach came in.
He wanted Jacques to get
back out on the ice.

The game needed to go on.

But Jacques said no.

"I won't play," Jacques said.

"Unless I can wear my mask."

The coach was very angry.

Outside the locker room,

the clock was ticking.

The players and fans were waiting

for the game to start again.

Finally, the coach made a decision.

"Okay," he said to Jacques.

"You can wear the mask this time."

Jacques skated back onto the ice.

He was wearing his mask.

Everyone was shocked.

They thought Jacques looked strange.

They thought he looked silly.

But then something great happened.

Jacques played so well that

the Canadiens won the game.

They won the next game too.

Jacques and the Canadiens

won eleven games in a row.

By then Jacques's cut had healed.

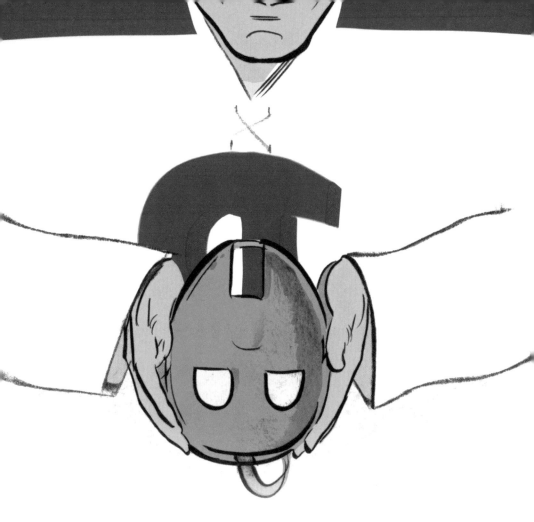

Lots of people were teasing him
about wearing the mask.

Jacques didn't care.

He liked his mask.

But his coach still didn't like it.

So, in the next game,

Jacques played without his mask.

The Canadiens lost.

The coach wanted to win.

The team wanted to win.

The fans wanted to win!

So the coach let Jacques

wear the mask again.

It worked!

The Canadiens started to win again.

They even won the Stanley Cup.

Soon, other goalies

started wearing masks.

Today all players wear helmets.

All goalies wear masks.

And we have a goalie named

Jacques Plante to thank!

# WHAT'S IN

# A NUMBER?

by Meg Braithwaite

Illustrations by Nick Craine

Only a few NHL players have worn the number 99.

Do you know who

the most famous one was?

Yes, it's Wayne Gretzky!

That number was special to Wayne.

Wayne's favourite hockey player
was Gordie Howe.

And Gordie wore number 9.

Wayne asked for number 9

whenever he could.

And he usually got it.

But then Wayne started

junior hockey.

The number 9 was already taken.

Oh no!

Wayne was sad.

So his coach said,

"Why not wear two 9s?"

"Good idea!" Wayne said.

He had 99 stitched on his sweater.

Lots of NHL players pick
numbers for special reasons.
Sometimes it's for the same
reason as Wayne.

They pick the numbers

their heroes wore.

Jonathan's favourite player
wore the number 19.
So Jonathan wears 19 too.

Sometimes players pick numbers that people in their family wore.

Auston's grandpa
played basketball in college.
So Auston wears 34,
just like his grandpa did.

Alex's grandma

played basketball at the Olympics.

So Alex wears 8 like she did.

But players choose numbers

for other reasons too.

Sidney picked the number 87
because he was born in 1987.

Jordin Tootoo's last name sounds

like "two-two."

So he wears the number 22.

But players can't always get
the numbers they want.

John couldn't use the number 19.

So he flipped it around to 91.

Russ couldn't get the number 9.

So he turned it upside down.

He wore a 6.

Mario did the same thing.

He wore 66 to honour Wayne Gretzky.

Pierre wanted the number 10.

But the number 10 was being used.

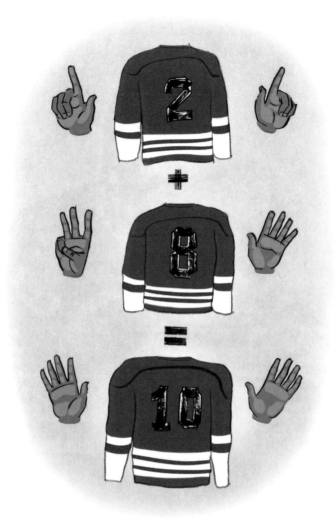

So Pierre chose 28.

Why?

Because 2 plus 8 equals 10.

Maurice chose a number
for his daughter.

She weighed nine pounds when
she was born.

So he chose the number 9.

But there's one number that
no hockey player will ever
wear again.

That's Wayne's number 99.

The NHL decided Wayne would

be the last one to wear it.

He was that good.

# What number would you choose if you were in the NHL?